More Praise for M.J. Clark

"M.J. Clark's helpful leadership guidance and thoughtful homework assignments definitely helped me to grow. I recommend M.J., her process, and the personal coaching experience to anyone who wants to challenge him or herself and find the tools to be successful in a leadership role!"
— **Diana L. Savage, Superintendent**
Bryan City Schools

"M.J. Clark gets you to recognize the 'true' you, and how that impacts your communication and interaction with others at work and in your personal life. M.J.'s leadership process allows you to learn things about yourself without having to beat yourself up about those things you could do better."
— **Carol Lingle, Former Sr. Human Resources Manager**
Waste Management, Inc.

"Being a novice to executive coaching and the leadership development process, I really wasn't sure what to expect from M.J. Clark. I have to say that my expectations were more than exceeded! I gained insight into behaviors, my own and those around me, which helped me determine what I needed to change about myself to obtain my personal and professional goals. I recommend this process and working with M.J. to anyone!"
— **Terri Brown, Manager, Marketing Services and Communications**
Elmer's Products, Inc.

"Everything M.J. Clark represents is honest, open, and founded on genuine concern for her fellow man. Anyone involved with M.J.'s leadership process gets incredible value for the money, a 'number one cheerleader,' and a very tender friend."
— **Amy DeShon, Former Executive Director**
Community Gardeners Association

Shut Up
And Lead:
A Communicator's Guide to Quiet Leadership

M.J. Clark, M.A., APR

Foreword by Bruce Cadwallader

Shut Up And Lead: A Communicator's Guide to Quiet Leadership makes a great gift, teaching tool, and/or self-help guide. For more information (including information on bulk purchases for friends, family, employees, or members of your group or organization), contact the author by email at mj@integratedleader.com or visit www.integratedleader.com.

Editing, design, and layout by Matt McGovern
www.700acres.com

Cover art by Katie Inverso Redinger
Inverso Creative, LLC

Table of Contents

Shut Up and Lead:
A Foreword

by Bruce Cadwallader

I WISH I HAD met someone like M.J. Clark 30 years ago, when I first set my tennis shoes on the brick-laden streets at Ohio University. I was scared, naive, and wimpy. Instead of embracing my college years, I cried like a baby when my parents dropped me off outside Washington Hall.

Yet I grew to be a quiet leader anyway. I studied hard, drank hard, and learned a lot about my fellow man in those dormitories. I was going to become a news photographer.

Then I took my first art class or two and fell out of love with the genre.

Then I listened to a professor—experience is a wonderful teacher, too—and pursued my hidden passion for writing instead. I found a job at the city desk of the student paper my sophomore year and applied for a position in residence life. All of a sudden, I was leading and not following. Eventually, I didn't want to leave those dormitories or that college. I still return, fondly.

In her book, *Shut Up and Lead*, M.J. reminds us all that sometimes we are not the smartest in the room, or the one who best portrays his passion, but often the best communicators know when to listen more than they speak. I learned that message early in my career as a newspaper reporter at three other Ohio newspapers.

I would routinely return to the newsroom in my first year at *The Columbus Dispatch* without enough "quote" fodder to write a decent column, mostly because I thought I had to run an interview instead of hosting one. Finally, an editor told me once as he tossed an empty notebook at my feet, "Fill these up, we'll buy you more!"

I began to listen more than I spoke. I began each interview with a more pleasant tone, a demeanor that said, "Yes, I'm interested in what you have to say!" even if I wasn't. I conquered spelling errors; errors in fact and omission. And I think I became a pretty good judge of a story, anyone's story.

Years later, I embraced public speaking and a run at the presidential ladder of a national journalism society. It was exposure to quiet leadership on a national scale. Even though I never became president of the Society of Professional Journalists, my failures helped reshape my character.

Back at *The Dispatch*, I wrote 5,500 bylined pieces before something tugging inside me said it was time to move on after a 27-year career. That's about the time I began working with M.J. Clark on a plan to set my feet on a different path.

My editor at the time, realizing it too, told me I was frequently "restless" about my future. My wife knew I was unhappy as well.

Ask yourself: What do other people see when they look into my mirror? More importantly, as M.J. points out, it's best to get to know yourself finally in those reflective moments and change the behavior or attitude that's getting in the way of your success.

Now, as senior director of a local public relations firm, I think I have overcome that fear of change: thanks to the concepts in this book and friends like M.J. who said, "Sure you can. You'd be good at that!"

With a boost of ego and a tweak or two of a resume, you too can make a change in your life if you want to.

I'm glad she was there for me.

I pray you read on and become a better "you" for doing so.

— Bruce Cadwallader, BSJ
(Ohio University 1983)

Dedication

TO MY FAMILY: THANK you, Bob, for loving me unconditionally. You are the most amazing man I know. Thank you, Carson and Connor, for challenging me to become more quiet, patient, loving, and forgiving. I thank God every day for choosing me to be your Mom.

Introduction

"THE PRESIDENT CALLED. SHE has an emergency to deal with at the office and can't be at today's luncheon," said the PRSA Programs Committee chair into the phone. "As president-elect, can you run the meeting?"

"Of course," I said, not realizing that this important luncheon would be the catalyst to changing my life and career in a profound way, one that would bring me closer to my true passion and allow me to marry my two loves: communications and leadership.

The speaker at the Public Relations Society of America luncheon that day was Steven L. Anderson, Ph.D., MBA, author of *The Call to Authenticity, Embracing Rebellion,* and *How to Create a World Class Company.* As Dr. Anderson discussed several leadership concepts framed by cognitive behavioral psychology, I was captivated by the material presented and knew immediately that this was what I wanted to do with my life.

When he finished his talk, I waited in line with others to say hello. When it was my turn, I stuck out my hand and enthusiastically said, "I'm M.J. Clark, and I want to be you when I grow up." Thus began a journey to who I am now, more my true self than ever before and happier and calmer than I ever imagined I could be.

When I met Steve, I believe I was finally ready to hear the message he had to give. Had I heard the same speech years earlier, I don't know that I would have been so struck by his words. But I was in the middle of a two-year master's degree program in organizational communication at The Ohio State University, and I was becoming keenly interested in neuroscience and the ways psychology influences our leadership and management abilities.

It was in the second year of this master's program, while I was still engaged with Steve in discussions about how we might work together, in which I found myself in the most profound state of dysfunction that I had ever been.

While attending Ohio State's program full-time, which also included conducting research and teaching classes, I was running my public relations consulting business, was president of the Central Ohio PRSA (a 400-member association), and was a wife and mother of two small boys. I was not dealing well with the added stress, and I believe I reached my ultimate capacity, the point at which I could no longer function effectively.

One day, while sitting alone entering data into a computer in an OSU research lab, tears began to flow down my face. I was truly shocked and had no idea why I was crying. But the tears continued, eventually to the point where I could no longer work. I called my advisor, the professor for whom I was entering the research data, and told him what happened. I asked him if I could just go home, because I wasn't getting anything done. He agreed and asked if I thought I should see one of the free counselors on campus. I said no and that I thought this was probably an isolated incident.

I was very wrong. These crying episodes began to come with more frequency, leaving me more and more confused. I finally took my advisor's advice and saw a campus counselor. It was there I learned that this was my body's way of letting me know it was under extreme stress. Although no one thing precipitated the onset of tears, which is what originally confounded me, it became apparent to me that the tears came when I was alone with my thoughts. This was a big lesson for me. I spent so much time doing, that I spent little time being. And being is what helps people process emotions, embrace creativity, and assess situations. When I was alone, I felt the full load I was carrying, and I was truly overwhelmed, which created tears.

I spoke to Steve about these tears, and he suggested I journal about what was going on. Although I was doing a lot of writing for school and was not very interested in doing more writing, I felt it was important to explore what was happening to me. This was the beginning of my journey to greater emotional intelligence, balance, and self-knowledge. And it was my great desire to improve my life that led to my decision to work for Steve at Integrated Leadership Systems.

When I began meeting with Steve, he was calm, assertive, balanced, and authentic. He spoke very slowly and was very thoughtful and creative. He challenged me, but also supported me. The more time I spent with him, the more I wanted to be like him. He gently told me one day that I talked too much and that I was living life at too fast a pace. He was right on both counts, and I was, and still am, truly grateful for the feedback he was courageous enough to give me. He has trained me as an executive coach, and I feel more balanced and more powerful as a result of his time and attention.

My hope for each of my readers is that this book helps you become more of your true self. I want you to learn from my mistakes and move closer to becoming a person who makes you proud, balanced, and truly happy. As you may have guessed, I am still on a journey. I will never be "done," but I know I have improved and will continue to do so.

> **"Never try to be better than someone else. But never stop working to become your best self."**
> **—John Wooden**

Chapter One

COVERING THE BASICS

"I CAN'T BELIEVE THAT conversation," she said to herself. "I wanted so much to impress the owner of that company, but I couldn't shut up. I think I said the same thing three times, in three different ways, right in a row. What does he think of me? I didn't let him speak. I didn't ask for his opinion. Why can't I control my mouth?!"

Does this self talk sound familiar? Most people who would label themselves good communicators talk too much. I know because I am one of those people, and I know a bunch of other communicators with the same challenge.

Based on great advice I got from a mentor to "shut up and lead," more or less, I have worked hard in the last several years to control my talking. I now give much more thought to what I share and when I share it, controlling the natural extrovert that I am. And I spend much more time listening to others, focusing on further developing patience and nurturing my sincere interest in others.

I'm certainly not "cured," and I slip up from time to time, and talk too much and occasionally interrupt others. This is something I will likely have to work on for years to come.

I now practice what I call "Quiet Leadership," which I define as leading through listening. There is also a book called *Quiet Leadership* by David Rock, but he defines the concept differently[1]. My idea of Quiet Leadership is that to lead more effectively, you can't be the one talking all the time. In fact, you must spend more time listening than talking. When you talk too much, people don't listen because they are getting a lot of unimportant information along with the important information. Instead, you must carefully choose what you share with others—only the most important information—so that when you speak, people actually listen.

I believe communicators are in a unique position in their organizations to affect great leadership change. When people don't know what to say, they turn to us: the public relations professionals, executive coaches, advertising executives, marketing gurus, human resources experts, lawyers, CEOs, media reporters, college professors, administrators, and other communicators. How we behave, which is how we teach those around us, most certainly affects the organizations in which we work and impacts the leaders within them at every level.

This book outlines the critical elements that I believe will take all communicators to the next stage in their careers and position communicators to be extremely influential in their organizations or in their own businesses. There is power in Quiet Leadership, and I want to share with you what I have learned over the years about how to lead effectively without doing all the talking.

First, we need to discuss some basics. I just mentioned that our behavior is how we teach those around us. We've heard parents say, and perhaps you have said, "Do what I say, not what I do." That's because people (especially children) pay much closer attention to what we do than what we say.

The results of a study in 1971 by Albert Mehrabian[2] concluded that there are three elements that make up face-to-face communication: words, tone of voice, and body language. These three elements, according to Mehrabian, account for our "liking" of the person relaying the message. Words account for 7%, tone of voice accounts for 38%, and body language accounts for 55% of the fondness we feel toward the speaker.

Further, the study showed that non-verbal elements convey feelings and attitude, especially when they do not match the words spoken. That means if words and body language do not match, the recipient of the message tends to believe the body language.

Picture someone you know, a male acquaintance, who is usually lively. Now envision him quietly sulking around an event or a party, looking at the floor, arms folded, with a sad expression on his face.

We might approach him and ask, "Are you okay? What's wrong?"

If he were to answer, "No; I'm fine. Just a little tired," would you believe him?

Body language is a pretty powerful indicator that something is not fine. And a sad expression says a little more to us than "I'm tired." We rely on body language to give us clues to what a person is not saying about his or her feelings at a given moment.

I want to stress that non-verbal elements do not convey the content of a message, but rather the feelings and conviction the speaker has about the message. In fact, when people lecture, nearly the entire message is conveyed orally, but non-verbal elements show the speaker's belief or passion about what he or she is saying. The more conviction the speaker has for a message, confirmed primarily through body language, the more we will like the person because he or she appears to be authentic.

Our behavior teaches others much more about us and how we feel at a given moment than our words. And yet communicators seem to worry little about their body language during interpersonal conversation. Of course, we all think a lot more about our body language when we are presenting something in front of an audience. But think about how much time we spend in one-on-one conversations as opposed to public speaking. All of those individual encounters create a picture of us that other people carry around with them, just like a child's photo in a parent's wallet. And when someone else asks for that person's opinion of you, he or she reflects on that picture when beginning the description.

This book is designed to help you give others your best picture—not a fake picture of how you want others to see you, but an authentic photo of who you are deep inside. A photo that shows your best you, as you work to become more and more your best self.

Chapter One — Key Points

- Quiet Leadership is leading through listening.

- To lead more effectively, you must spend more time listening than talking.

- How we behave, which is how we teach those around us, affects our organizations and the leaders within them at every level.

- Albert Mehrabian's study found that when a person is talking to us, our "liking" of the person, or the fondness we feel toward him or her, is accounted for by his or her words (7%), tone of voice (38%), and body language (55%).

- If words and body language do not match, according to Mehrabian, the recipient of the message (or listener) tends to believe the body language.

- Even though non-verbal elements are critical in message delivery, they do not convey the content of a message, but rather the feelings and conviction the speaker has about the message.

- All of our individual encounters create a picture of us that other people carry around with them, just like a child's photo in a parent's wallet.

Notes

> **"Live as if you were to die tomorrow.**
> **Learn as if you would live forever."**
> **—Gandhi**

Chapter Two

THE CHANGING FIELD OF COMMUNICATIONS

WHILE AT A BROWN bag luncheon sponsored by the Legal Marketing Association, a discussion ensued about our changing communications field. I shared that although many communicators like to practice forecasting to help their organizations stay ahead in their industry, it's almost impossible to do nowadays. The communications landscape continues to change, primarily because of new technology that continues to amaze and delight and burden us.

Although it's difficult to keep abreast of all the latest technological advancements, it's critical to our careers. New tools that communicators can employ continue to come forth, further confusing our clients or companies and leaving many of us communicators to wonder how we will most effectively incorporate the latest trend into our strategic plans. To avoid feeling overwhelmed, I often think of each new advancement as another tool in my tool belt that I can choose to use or not, knowing that not every new tool must be used, regardless of what the "experts" tell us.

Some newer technologies, such as particular social media sites or new tech toys, may not be in your comfort zone. Instead of feeling you must give each new site or technology a try, you may read about how people use it for business purposes and then decide if you want to jump in or wait a bit longer. Sometimes it pays to wait, to see others work out the kinks so you can learn from them, and sometimes we lament being a late adopter because we seem a little behind the times compared to our competitors. Either way, the choice is ours, and we learn from each of these choices.

As a communicator, the most damaging element of so much new technology is the obvious sacrifice we are making to superior interpersonal communication. Our social skills can't help but suffer when we spend the majority of our time linking, friending, tweeting, following, texting, emailing, and IM-ing one another. Those who are passive find it easier than ever to send someone an email or text instead of confronting a problem or communicating face-to-face. Even hand-written notes have become uncommon. My nephew recently told me that my advice to send a hand-written thank you note following a job interview is what landed him the job. His new boss told him that his was the only note he received from the group of job candidates he recently interviewed.

As an executive coach, I find that more than ever I am asked to help executives improve their interpersonal communication skills. I can tell you with confidence that the best way to improve communication skills is to understand ourselves better and to be courageous and put ourselves in situations that scare and challenge us. It is only through repeated practice of those things with which we struggle that we improve and eventually master those skills.

With the crutches of new technology, it's easier than ever simply to avoid what we don't do well. But avoidance is merely a Band-Aid on a wound. You will encounter the same scary situation in the future, and you will realize you are just as unprepared as you were the last time, unless you make a decision to improve and take the steps necessary to make it happen.

Chapter Two — Key Points

- Although it's difficult to keep abreast of all the latest technological advancements, it's critical to our careers.

- One of the most damaging by-products of so much new technology is the sacrifice of superior interpersonal communication.

- People who are passive find it easier than ever to send someone an e-mail or text instead of confronting a problem or communicating face-to-face.

- The best way to improve communication skills is to understand ourselves better and to put ourselves in situations that scare and challenge us.

Notes

> "Better to have people think you are a fool than to open your mouth and remove all doubt."
> —Mark Twain

Chapter Three

LISTENING TO OTHERS

HERE'S THE PART ABOUT shutting up. As a communicator, you probably find that you spend much of your time talking.

We are usually drawn to some aspect of the communications field because we like to interact with others. So many communicators say, "I'm a 'people person.'" As communicators, we usually enjoy helping people understand things, and we feel we are good at explaining things. The downside is that we often spend much more time talking than we do listening.

Because people learn more from what we do than from what we say, it makes sense for us to listen intently to others so that . . .

1. We can understand them more thoroughly and act with their best interests in mind.

2. We can model this behavior so others will listen to us more attentively.

3. We have more credibility when we do speak because we
   have more information from them with which to draw
   conclusions and give appropriate suggestions.

I used to find that when I was nervous, I would say the same
thing a few times in a variety of ways. I wanted to make sure the person
understood, and I wanted to make sure he or she thought I was offering
good information, so I would explain it to death. When I started to
realize I was doing this, the knowledge of it alone didn't immediately
solve the problem. I would observe myself doing it yet again and then
would walk away thinking, "Why the heck did I do that again?!" The
more I learned about myself, the more I realized it happened only when
I really wanted to impress someone.

Think about what you just read. When I really wanted to impress
someone, I would talk too much, which resulted in the opposite of
my goal!

People are not generally impressed, of course, by how much you
say. In fact, when you over-explain something, the listener may feel you
are being condescending.

What you say and how you say it makes much more of an
impact, which is the whole idea behind Quiet Leadership. By listening
carefully to others, what you say will be much more thoughtful and
knowledgeable. It can be well tailored to the listener, once you have
a clear understanding of the person with whom you are talking. So to
impress others, we must listen.

Many people think listening just comes naturally. It doesn't.
Many women I know think their husbands don't listen well. These same
women talk at their husbands all day long—not *with* them, but *at* them.

If someone constantly talks and doesn't practice listening themselves, how can he or she expect the same measure of respect in return?

If you feel that someone is not listening to you, then practice not talking. The more quiet you become, the more curiosity this raises in the person you want so desperately to listen to you. It is more likely that this person will listen to you respectfully when you begin choosing only the most important things to share instead of every little nugget that pops into your head. When the other person begins to learn that you are choosing what to share carefully, and that these bits of information truly are important, only then will you have his or her attention.

Have you ever been in a conversation with a person who is typing on a computer, retrieving a text message, or reading something while you are talking? Or perhaps you are the person who does these things while in a conversation. It's disrespectful and hurtful to the other person. It's not okay.

I remember when, early in my career, I used to use technology and other things around me to send non-verbal messages to others. I was working with another female with whom I didn't care to be friends. She would come into my office and talk for long periods. I didn't want to hurt her feelings, and I didn't want to listen to her either. So when she came in, I would type on my computer, answer the phone if it rang, read things on my desk, and act as though I was just barely listening to her. It was very passive-aggressive behavior, and I did so just hoping she would "take the hint." Well she didn't. And I didn't have the guts to address her directly and tell her what I needed from her.

It would have been more respectful for me to say, "Susan, I just can't spend this amount of time talking during my work day. I have too much work to do. I appreciate that you have stopped by, but I'm going to have to get back to work now." And then I could stand up and walk her to my door. The way I used to do it, our conversations always did end with me walking her to my door, but it was after torturous amounts of wasted time while I mustered the courage to stand up.

So we can choose to tell others respectfully and assertively that we don't have the time to listen to them. But how do we listen when we really do want to hear someone?

The most important thing is to maintain good eye contact. Our eye contact shows the other person that he or she has our attention. In addition, leaning in slightly helps him or her feel you are engaged. Job recruiters often coach prospective candidates to lean in slightly during interviews. It may feel awkward at first, but doing so gives the impression of engagement and interest in the conversation. If you find it too uncomfortable to look others directly in the eyes, then practice looking at the nose instead. Others will not know you are looking at their noses; trust me. I have practiced this with others at close range and have been assured that it appears I'm looking them in the eyes. After you try this for a while, you can slowly work up to alternating looking at the nose, and then the eyes, and then the nose again. Eventually you may become more comfortable with looking just at a person's eyes.

When listening, it's helpful to give verbal feedback that shows you hear the person. I used to get very frustrated when talking on the phone with my husband because he would not say a word. When I would say, "Hello, are you hearing me? You're not saying anything," he would respond, "I'm just listening." Finally, I said to him one day, "Please just grunt or something to let me know you're still out there!"

We need that human feedback. We need to know the person with whom we are taking the time to communicate is actively listening and understanding what we are sharing. Instead of grunting, I would recommend saying things like "Mm, hmm," "Yes." "Wow!" Then, later in the conversation, take them back to comments they made earlier when you are making a point.

For example, you might say to your listener:

"As you said earlier, it would be good to get my certification, so I think I will take your advice and sign up for the class."

"I like the point you made about becoming certified."

"When you mentioned becoming certified earlier, it made me think of other things I need to do."

When you can repeat things the speaker has said, because you are listening intently, your conversational partner will feel respected and understood.

Another listening technique is to rephrase what the person is saying, such as "So are you saying that getting certified would help me in my career?" This shows the person you are trying hard to understand the message he or she is trying to relay. Many times, when I first started to use that technique, the person to whom I was listening would say, "No, that's not what I'm saying at all." That'll teach me, huh?

Active listening takes practice, and you have to keep trying before you become really efficient at listening and understanding others. But having the courage to make an effort is the first step.

Something else to try is to mirror the person's emotions. If a female speaker is talking about how she feels about something, try to come up with a word that you think sums up her feelings, even if she has not used that particular word. For example, if she is describing a situation where she is just banging her head against the wall, and she feels she is getting nowhere and nobody wants to help her, you can say, "That sounds so frustrating." Often times the speaker will say, "Yes! That's exactly it! I'm so frustrated I could just scream."

Letting someone know you understand the feeling he or she is experiencing is powerful, even if you can't say you have had the very same experience. It's the empathy that counts.

Chapter Three — Key Points

- It's important to listen intently to others so (1) we can understand them more thoroughly and act with their best interests in mind, (2) we can model this behavior so others will listen to us more attentively, and (3) we have more credibility when we do speak because we have more information from them with which to draw conclusions and give appropriate suggestions.

- When you over-explain something, in an effort to impress someone with your knowledge, the listener may feel you are being condescending.

- If you feel that someone is not listening to you, then practice not talking. It is more likely the person will listen to you when you share only the most important things instead of every thought that pops into your head.

- Keys to attentive listening:

  1. Maintain good eye contact

  2. Give verbal feedback that shows you hear the person

  3. Repeat what the person is saying

  4. Mirror the person's emotions

Notes

> "When you are content simply to be
> yourself and don't compare or compete,
> everyone will respect you."
> —Lao-tzu

Chapter Four

PRACTICING ASSERTIVENESS

AGGRESSIVE PEOPLE WHO SEEK to control others and passive people who let others control them do not make good leaders. To lead, we must learn to say what we feel and stand up for our rights. Quiet Leadership is not about sitting by silently. It's about calmly sticking up for ourselves, patiently seeking to understand others more thoroughly, and allowing them to understand and trust us. When we open up in this way, we model authentic communication and foster teamwork.

To lead as a communicator, we must exhibit both confidence and vulnerability. We must strongly believe in our abilities, but we must also appear real and human and fallible to those who follow. We will make mistakes. And that's okay; it's necessary for our ultimate success.

To become more assertive, it's importance to practice. When we are not very assertive, but more passive, we should practice in safe places. We don't want to walk up to our bosses or important clients tomorrow and practice assertiveness. Important conversations with people who are critical to our success must wait for a fine-tuned approach.

So how do you initiate an assertive conversation? There are three simple steps you can use:

1. Describe the behavior.

2. Explain how it makes you feel.

3. Explain the changes you would like to see.

Let's look at each one of these in turn.

First, you describe the behavior. We lead the conversation with a description of the behavior (and not a personal comment) because it's difficult to refute what you and the other person both see happening. To do this, you would say something such as, "I have noticed that when I speak up in the staff meetings, you roll your eyes, which causes our co-workers to laugh."

When you then explain how it makes you feel, the second step, you might say something such as, "When you roll your eyes, it makes me feel ridiculed and criticized." We use the construct, "When you do X, it makes me feel Y," because the other person cannot argue with how you feel. Other people are not in charge of our emotions; we own our feelings. The person you are confronting may say in reply, "You shouldn't feel that way!" and you can respond with, "Well, I do." Others cannot dictate what we should or should not feel. We feel what we feel—end of story.

The last step, saying what you would like to see happen moving forward, is the step often missed, which only creates a situation where the same scenario may play out again a few months later. What you might say for this step is, "I really don't want this to happen again, because I don't like feeling this way. In the future, I would prefer that if you don't like a comment I make in the staff meeting, you bring it to me privately and refrain from rolling your eyes or indicating with other body language what you may be feeling in the moment. Will you agree to do this?"

I think it's important to end with a question to which the other person will have to answer yes or no. If the other person says no, then I would listen to what he or she says and continue to try to reach an agreement on what to do in the future. If the person says yes, and then you see the same infraction in the future, you can approach him or her and say, "I noticed in today's meeting that you rolled your eyes at one of my comments. I felt ridiculed again, and I asked you not to do this in the future. You agreed to come to me directly when you didn't agree with a comment, but that didn't happen. Can we talk about this?"

When you confront someone, it's important not to sound accusatory or label the behavior as wrong. The person has a reason for what he or she is doing and may not even realize that it's hurtful to you. Don't call the person names or allow yourself to lose control. If you are gentle and go out of your way not to make the person defensive, the meeting has a better chance of going smoothly. In addition to listening intently to what he or she says to you, it is also critical to stay focused. You came with a message, and you must be strong and say what you planned to say so you don't end up acquiescing and simply allowing the behavior to continue.

There are also many small opportunities to practice your assertiveness. For instance, when you are in a line for coffee and someone cuts in front of you, in a very kind voice you can practice saying, "Excuse me, I think I was next." Or if that doesn't seem very challenging, perhaps you can confront someone you love who is hurting you in some way. For instance, feel free to steal what I recently said to my pre-teen son: "Please don't begin or end your sentences with the word 'Duh!' It makes me feel like you think I'm stupid, and it makes me feel disrespected. I want us to talk to each other respectfully, so let's continue to practice having conversations without using that word. Will you practice this with me?"

If you are more on the aggressive side, try to practice asking questions such as "What can we do together to solve this problem?" or "How can I be a better (boss, father, friend, wife) to you?" or "Tell me more about that."

Approaching others as equal partners and being more aware of when you are trying to control and direct will help you begin to chip away at the personal characteristics you wish to change.

Most people are not perfectly assertive; they fall on the passive or aggressive ends of the scale. It's a very comfortable place to be on one end or the other of this scale. You generally know what to expect. Being assertive feels very unsteady, even though that's exactly where we are best served. When you decide to be more assertive, you will experience awkward moments, and things will not come out of your mouth perfectly at times. You will make mistakes. You will sometimes get responses you don't expect because you are approaching others in a new way. Just know this, and do it anyway. It's the only way to improve.

Chapter Four — Key Points

- Aggressive people who seek to control others and passive people who let others control them do not make good leaders.

- Quiet Leadership is about calmly sticking up for ourselves, patiently seeking to understand others more thoroughly, and allowing them to understand and trust us.

- To lead as a communicator, we must exhibit both confidence and vulnerability.

- There are three steps to use to initiate an assertive conversation:

    1. Describe the behavior

    2. Explain how it makes you feel

    3. Explain the changes you would like to see

- Examples of the three steps:

    1. "I have noticed that when I speak up in the staff meetings, you roll your eyes, which causes our co-workers to laugh."

    2. "When you do this, it makes me feel ridiculed and criticized."

    3. "In the future, I would prefer that if you don't like a comment I make in the staff meeting, you bring it to me privately and refrain from rolling your eyes or indicating with other body language what you may be feeling in the moment. Will you agree to do this?"

- Look for small, safe opportunities to practice your assertiveness.

- When you decide to be more assertive, you will experience awkward moments, and things will not come out of your mouth perfectly at times. You will make mistakes, and that's okay. It's how we learn.

Notes:

> "That you may retain your self-respect, it is
> better to displease others by doing what you
> know is right, than to temporarily please them by
> doing what you know is wrong."
> —William Boetcker

Chapter Five

FOCUSING ON CHARACTER

WITH AN UNDERGRADUATE DEGREE in public relations, I've spent a good deal of time focusing on the outside of people. When I would prep someone for a media interview, I thought about how he or she would appear. Is his hair combed? Will the suit look good on camera? Will she fidget? Will she be able to deliver the key messages? What facial expressions will work best?

After earning a master's degree in organizational communication, it became clearer to me that focusing on the outside is not what serves people best. In fact, it's the easy way out. It's easy to control what others see.

I can look fantastic, but does it mean I'm "together?" No.

Does a fancy title in a company mean I'm a leader? No.

What matters most and what gets us ahead is focusing on what's on the inside. But it's awfully messy in there, and it can be scary to look at it. Many of us have avoided dealing with it for a long, long time. So what's there now is based on habits reinforced over decades, and we can't simply flip a switch and make all those bad habits go away.

To be the best person we can be, we must focus on character. And the flaws we find when we look at ourselves with a critical eye must be addressed. We can't attack all the problems at once. That would be overwhelming. But we can work on them over time, focusing initially on the ones that bother us the most or are the most counter-productive to the goals we wish to achieve. We will likely have setbacks along the way. It will not be easy.

To become the person you most want to be takes work. You must challenge yourself to change on the inside so you can become different on the outside.

What does it feel like to look in the mirror? Can you look at yourself, at the one staring back at you, and honestly say out loud, "I love you?"

I know many people who find this exercise extremely difficult. I first discovered this when I gave a speech about affirmations to the Columbus, Ohio, chapter of eWomenNetwork. I recommended saying, "I love you" into a mirror as a way to foster self-love. Many of the women in the audience bristled at the suggestion. One of the women said her therapist had recommended the same thing to her, and she found herself crying during her first attempt. Why can't we simply love ourselves, warts and all?

What parts of you do you not like? How committed are you to changing those parts?

As an executive coach, I can tell you that loving yourself is very tough for some people. There are parts of each of us that we would rather not own. We push them away, like sweeping dust under a rug. And when we finally lift up the rug to see all the yucky mess we have accumulated over the years, it's daunting and overwhelming to think about cleaning it all up. But if we want to be the best we can be, it's critical to clean the mess—not all in one day, but in small pieces over time, with patience and love for ourselves.

Many people think they just are who they are. They do not feel empowered to change who they have been for so many years. But YOU are in charge of you! You show others who you are every moment of every day, with each decision you make, each word you speak, and each action you take. If you change your thoughts and your behaviors, you change you. So who do you want to be?

Chapter Five — Key Points

- Focusing on the outside is not what serves people best; it's the easy way out. It's easy to control what others see. What matters most and what gets us ahead is focusing on what's on the inside.

- What's inside of us now is based on habits reinforced over decades. And we can't simply flip a light switch and make all those bad habits go away.

- The flaws we find when we look at ourselves with a critical eye must be addressed over time.

- Try this exercise: say "I love you" into a mirror as a way to foster self-love.

- You show others who you are every moment of every day, with each decision you make, each word you speak, and each action you take.

Notes

> "I believe people are about as happy as they
> make up their minds to be."
> —Abraham Lincoln

Chapter Six

CONTROLLING YOUR THOUGHTS

WHAT WE THINK GREATLY impacts how we behave. It's not enough just to think positively. You have to believe what you think. If you "try" to think positively, and yet your inner voice doesn't truly believe that you deserve to succeed, you will never reach your goals.

I often tell clients to make affirmation cards, using 3x5 index cards, and I use these cards myself, reading them several times throughout each day. Affirmation cards are a tool to help you think differently. They are written in the first person (using "I" statements) and written as if the ideal situation already exists.

For instance, I have coached individuals who struggle with anger management. An affirmation that someone in this situation might write would be "I am the calm in the storm," or "I take time throughout each day to breathe calmly" or "I always respond in a calm manner in the workplace." For someone struggling with self-esteem issues, an affirmation might be "I am lovable and capable." It could be "People love me just as I am" or "I am caring, funny, and thoughtful." If you want to lose weight, an affirmation might be, "I exercise every day because I love feeling fit" or "I am thin, and I look incredible."

Affirmations can be written for both your professional and personal life. Often the changes we hope to make are the same or very similar in both arenas. They are sometimes hard to detect without some reflection, but if you have a quick temper or low self-esteem, it usually affects you as a person, not just as a lawyer or as a mother or as a friend. If you can write the affirmations specifically for your business and personal needs, you can focus more clearly on the precise behavior you seek to change.

Reading affirmations many times daily will reprogram your thinking. After weeks or months of this exercise, depending on how often you read them, you will see that when a situation arises that reflects an affirmation you have written, the affirmation will come to mind without referring to the card. Affirmations are positive self-talk that, over time, become healthy thinking habits.

The theory behind affirmations is that if you read them every day or throughout each day, and they really are not your current situation, you will feel compelled to do something about it. It creates something called "cognitive dissonance."

When you believe one thing, but the reality is something else, it bothers your mind, so you attempt to make your belief and reality match. For instance, when you think you are smart enough to have a college degree, and yet every time someone asks you where you went to college, you have to admit that you did not go to college, that will bother you. If you have to keep admitting that to people, and you assume they are judging you as not being smart when you feel that you are, you will eventually find a way to go to college.

What do you want to change about yourself? Who do you want to be? Do you want to lose weight, control your temper, feel respected by others, feel more loved? Take a moment now to create a set of 3x5 affirmation cards for yourself.

Chapter Six — Key Points

–   What we think greatly impacts how we behave.

–   Affirmation cards are a tool to help you think differently. They are written in the first person (using "I" statements) and written as if the ideal situation already exists.

–   Examples of affirmations:

    1. I am the calm in the storm.

    2. I take time throughout each day to breathe calmly.

    3. I am lovable and capable.

    4. People love me just as I am.

    5. I exercise every day because I love feeling fit.

    6. I am thin, and I look incredible.

–   Affirmations are positive self-talk that, over time, become healthy thinking habits.

–   "Cognitive dissonance" is when you believe one thing, but reality is something else, so it bothers your mind and you attempt to make your belief and reality match.

Notes

"Saying 'yes' to more things than we can actually manage to be present for with integrity and ease of being is in effect saying 'no' to all those things and people and places we have already said 'yes' to, including, perhaps, our own well-being."
—John Kabat-Zinn

Chapter Seven
CARING FOR YOURSELF

LEADERSHIP BEGINS WITH THE ability to care for your "self" in mind, body, and soul.

Caring for Your Mind

Do you have a best friend, or more than one? Do you have someone in your life to whom you could tell anything? Do you keep a journal, where you can record the thoughts you didn't even know you had until the pen began to write? These are some of the ways we care for our minds and address outside stresses.

I started meditating about 10 years ago. And at times when my life is very busy, it's a challenge to continue this important activity. When I say, "meditate," it may cause you to envision someone in a complicated yoga position, chanting, with thumbs and first fingers locked in an upside-down "OK" position. I don't know about you, but I find yoga positions especially uncomfortable and being in one does not generally make me feel calm. For my not-very-flexible readers, I want you to open your mind to think of meditation as an activity that is comfortable to you and a process you can mostly control.

I want to share with you how I approach meditation. First, I don't use music. As much as I love music, I find even music without words to be incredibly distracting during meditation. I get in a very comfortable position, usually sitting in a chair with an upright back with my feet flat on the floor. This may sound simple to you, but because I'm only 5'2", finding a chair that is close enough to the floor so that my feet can be comfortably flat can be a challenge! (It's helpful to think intently about these simple things that will make you most relaxed.)

I close my eyes, and I work to clear my mind of thoughts. To do this, I envision a light. I like to think of my light as God. I usually think the word "one," but you can choose any word that speaks to you, such as calm, peace, or love. To me, "one" represents my oneness with God and it makes me feel one with the universe. I sit in silence, seeing my God light, and I repeat the word "one" in my head for 10 to 20 minutes, depending on how much time I have available for the activity.

When I first began to meditate, my "to do" list would come to mind, over and over again. Each time, I had to gently push those thoughts to the side and again focus on my light and my word. Meditation takes practice. You don't just sit down and do this activity for 20 minutes. The first time, you may be able to do it for only two or three minutes. It will seem much longer than it actually is. You must practice to work up to 10 or 20 minutes.

So what does meditation do for us? Research suggests that meditation may be an effective intervention for cardiovascular disease[3]; anxiety and panic disorder[4]; chronic pain[5]; substance abuse[6]; reduction of psychological distress and symptoms of distress for cancer patients[7]; and reduction of medical symptoms in both clinical and non-clinical populations[8].

We inherited from our ancestors the fight or flight response to life threatening situations. The up side is that this response allows us to act quickly and reflexively so we can survive threatening situations without having to think about it. We get an adrenaline dump that helps us attack any problem quickly. The down side is that the adrenaline also quickens the pulse, raises blood pressure, and speeds breathing. This reflexive response lowers the ability to think clearly. It also slows decision-making and complex problem solving skills.

If we were in great danger, as our ancestors often were daily, all of the effects of an adrenaline dump would be very helpful. Unfortunately, this fight or flight response is now inappropriately triggered in our modern lives when our bosses confront us, when we get cut off in traffic, or when our teenagers disobey us.

If we are unsure as to how to deal with these situations, stress is prolonged, which can lead to serious health problems.

We don't normally think about breathing; we just do it. But breathing deeply can be very helpful in reducing stress when you don't have time for a meditation session. I suggest that you find time to breathe deeply throughout the day, and actually schedule it if necessary. Most people who are under a lot of stress or tension breathe shallowly, up in the chest or throat area. This is what causes hyperventilation during a severe anxiety attack.

It is often more helpful to focus on aerobic breathing, which involves your stomach. Place your hands on your abdomen, and as you breathe in through your nose, you will see and feel your stomach expand out. When you release the breath slowly through your mouth, your stomach will deflate. When you breathe deeply in this way, you are naturally bringing in more oxygen and activating energy in your body.

Try this: set your intention to take 10 deep breaths once every hour. (If necessary, set a timer to help you remember.) It will only take a minute, but the health rewards will be tenfold.

Caring for Your Body

An interesting study was done by several researchers[9] to test how stress affects the immune system. The researchers recorded the immunity levels of a group of students participating in the study. Then they divided the group into three smaller groups.

They asked students in the first group to go into separate, identical rooms and write on pieces of paper any random information that popped into their heads. They asked students in the second group to go into separate, identical rooms and write about painful personal episodes they had never shared with another person, and to record the hurt carried around because it was never resolved. The third group went into separate, identical rooms and received the same instruction as the second group, but instead of writing their episodes down on paper, they talked about them into a tape recorder.

The scientists then re-measured the immunity levels of all the students. The first group showed no change. The second group showed noticeable increases in the functioning of their immune systems. The third group's levels outdid that of the second group, showing even more positive effects.

At Integrated Leadership Systems, we ask all of our executive coaching clients to keep a journal to help them process some of the challenges in their lives, similar to what some in the second group may have been writing about.

The study suggests writing in a reflective way may be good for your overall health, but that speaking about personal pain is even more powerful in providing overall health benefits. There is power and health in the process of executive coaching, and an added health benefit by incorporating journaling on a regular basis.

We often know we are under stress and still don't take steps— such as journaling, or talking with friends, or changing things about our lives—to address it. Small changes in behavior can lead to profound health effects. Just ignoring the stress can often lead to tragedy.

I bought the house I live in now from a realtor named John. He was an excellent realtor, taking our calls at any time, showing houses on evenings or weekends, and generally trying to please us, his clients, in any way he could. Several months after he worked with us, he called me to ask for help.

"My doctor has told me for years that I need either to change the way I do my job or change careers entirely," John said. "He said I am under way too much stress, and yet I find it impossible to change things about my current job. So I think maybe I should look for a job in another industry. Would you help me?"

For the next couple of months, I helped John revamp his resume for another industry. We did mock interviews and met regularly to discuss his progress. After all the work he did, he was interviewing and I thought he was well on the way to a new career.

A few months later, John died of a massive heart attack. He was in his 50s. We all talk about managing stress, but John's death had a profound impact on how I live my life and how I teach stress management to business people.

Sometimes our bodies are smarter than we are. We need only to listen to them.

How do you care for yourself—a deep-tissue massage, a walk on the beach, an hour of silence in a church pew, a chat with a dear friend?

We often feel selfish when we take time for ourselves.

How often do you put yourself at the very bottom of your to do list? To be the best you can be for all the others in your life—your family, your friends, your clients or customers, your business partners— you need to take care of yourself first. The more you care for you, the happier you feel, the healthier you are, and the more positively you interact with all those you seek to serve in your life.

Many of us are truly surprised when we yell at our kids, cry unexpectedly, or continually feel like we are fighting illness. These are signs that we are not taking care of ourselves. When we don't deal with stress, or don't confront people assertively, it builds up inside of us like a volcano. Eventually, most people erupt.

But what generally happens is we erupt on someone who doesn't deserve it, such as our kids, or spouses, or best friends, because those people are safe. We know they love us and will still be there for us after we get it all out. Alternatively, if a supervisor's unreasonable demands cause stress, and we erupt on him or her, we may not have a job at the end of the day.

However, if we assertively and gently confront both business and personal problems in our lives as they occur, the buildup goes away, and the volcano becomes dormant. If we can interact with others peacefully and professionally and take the time to process our emotions regularly, then we can forestall illness with a high immunity level that results from this emotional stability.

Caring for Your Soul

Why are you on this earth? Is it to work 9 to 5, seven days a week, 365 days a year at a job you can't stand so you can collect a paycheck to feed your family or yourself? You were created with special talents for a purpose. Have you paid enough attention to discover your purpose, to live your purpose, to best utilize your talents while you are alive?

There is no way to describe with words how incredible it feels to wake up every day and do what you know you were put on this earth to do. And yet, I have met hundreds of people who continue to work at jobs that don't feed their souls. One person comes to mind immediately.

Brad was a participant in a workshop I was facilitating. I asked participants to identify their passions: that one thing that spoke to them on the deepest level and made them feel most alive. When it was Brad's turn to share his thoughts, he said deep sea diving was his passion.

"When I'm under the water, I feel so alive," he said. "I love the ocean. I love underwater life and plants. I would absolutely LOVE to wake up every day and know I could be in the ocean, to know that I could share my love of diving with others, first timers, who have no idea what they're missing. That would feel amazing."

I asked what he did for a living.

"I'm an accountant," he answered.

The room erupted in laughter.

"I'm good at accounting, but I don't absolutely love it," Brad said. "I'm just good with numbers, so I thought that made sense as a career."

"What would be the risk involved in pursuing deep sea diving as a career?" I asked.

Brad then began to identify all of the reasons he felt he could not pursue his dream.

"I would have to live on the coast. I would have to move my family. I might not be able to run such a business effectively. My family might think I'm crazy. I'd have to leave my friends."

"What would be the reward?" I asked.

"Oh my gosh," he said. "It would be everything! I would be so happy! What an amazing life that would be. I can't even imagine it."

Today, Brad is an accountant . . . and that breaks my heart. When my parents told me I could be anything I wanted to be, I believed them. And I believe it for my clients. Anything can be achieved, if you want it passionately enough.

How passionate are you about your goals? If you are not passionate about your current goals, perhaps it's time to create some new ones that truly speak to you.

When we spend energy making up a hundred excuses for why we can't do something, we are merely reacting, usually to fear. When we, instead, spend time pursuing a goal or dream about which we are passionate, that passion fuels action. Instead of passively letting circumstances in the world dictate our futures, passion fuels the desire to make positive change, and that causes action toward the goal.

When your soul is fed by pursuing your passion, you become excited, happier, and more focused. In that pursuit, you are becoming who you are supposed to be.

Chapter Seven — Key Points

Caring for Your Mind

–   Meditation may be an effective intervention for: cardiovascular disease, anxiety and panic disorder, chronic pain, substance abuse, reduction of psychological distress and symptoms of distress for cancer patients, and reduction of medical symptoms in both clinical and non-clinical populations.

–   The fight or flight response we inherited from our ancestors is now inappropriately triggered in our modern lives when our bosses confront us, when we get cut off in traffic, or when our teenagers disobey us. If we are unsure how to deal with these situations, stress is prolonged and can lead to serious health problems.

–   Breathing deeply can be very helpful in reducing stress when you don't have time to meditate. Find time to breathe deeply throughout the day.

Caring for Your Body

–   A research study suggests writing in a reflective way may be good for your overall health, but that speaking about personal pain is even more powerful in providing overall health benefits.

–   Small changes in behavior can lead to profound health effects. Just ignoring the stress can often lead to tragedy.

–   To be the best you can be for all the others in your life—your family, your friends, your clients or customers, your business partners—you need to take care of yourself first.

–   If we can interact with others in a peaceful, professional manner and take time to process our emotions regularly, then we can forestall illness with a high immunity level that results from this emotional stability.

Caring for Your Soul

– You were created with special talents for a purpose. Have you paid enough attention to discover your purpose?

– When we spend energy making up a hundred excuses for why we can't do something, we are merely reacting (usually to fear). When we, instead, spend time pursuing goals or dreams that we are passionate about, that passion fuels action.

Notes

"I am not bound to win, but I am bound to be true. I am not bound to succeed, but I am bound to live by the light that I have. I must stand with anybody that stands right, stand with him while he is right, and part with him when he goes wrong."
—Abraham Lincoln

Chapter Eight

CHOOSING ASSOCIATES CAREFULLY

PSYCHOLOGIST JOHN CACIOPPO, DIRECTOR of the Center for Cognitive and Social Neuroscience at the University of Chicago, "uncovered links between involvement in a distressing relationship and hikes in stress hormones to levels that damage certain genes that control virus-fighting cells," Daniel Goleman writes about Cacioppo's research in his book on social intelligence[10]. Cacioppo is now working on figuring out which neural pathways create this problem. For now, we need only realize that being involved in a distressing relationship causes stress that damages cells that fight viruses. That's not good.

Goleman also describes in his book a research study that concludes that emotions can be contagious. When we surround ourselves with upbeat people, we often are more so ourselves. And just the opposite is true—when we surround ourselves with sad people, it can affect our emotional states in a negative way.

Life is too short to spend time with people who view the world through cynical eyes, sap the energy from you, think only of themselves, and can't share meaningful conversation. Spending your time with intelligent, good humored, active, productive, insightful others who listen carefully and love you with all your warts motivates and uplifts you. And of course, you must choose to be this type of person if you wish to attract others with these characteristics to you.

I remember a family friend, Martha, to whom I spent a good deal of time listening when I lived at home in Wisconsin. She always seemed to have a problem to share, and she was always sad. I felt sorry for her, and I truly wanted to support her.

When I moved to another state, Martha started to write to me. (She wrote letters, which involved using a pen to write messages on paper, and then mailed the message in a stamped envelope to me. This is how we communicated in the olden days, before cell phones and computers and Facebook.) We shared letters back and forth for quite a while. One day, my boyfriend was at my apartment. He saw Martha's letter sitting on my table and asked who she was. I told him, and he asked if he could read the letter.

After reading it, he said, "That's the most depressing letter I've ever read."

"Oh my gosh," I said. "That's a really positive letter, compared to the others I've gotten."

He was shocked. He told me I should stop writing to her because her horrible letters were going to affect my outlook negatively. I slowed down my correspondence with her until we finally stopped writing to each other altogether. My boyfriend was right. Not getting her letters any more really helped me be more cheerful. I didn't realize how sad those letters made me feel until I no longer received them.

Although I truly have compassion for all human beings, and I'm sincerely grateful for each person with whom I come in contact, I am also very careful now to surround myself with friends and business associates who challenge and support me. Friends and business partners are crucial to success. Spending time with those who communicate authentically with us and challenge us to stretch ourselves are the key to our growth and confidence.

I did not know it back then, when I made the decision to end my correspondence with Martha, but I suspect now that Cacioppo is probably correct that my choice was a healthy one.

Chapter Eight — Key Points

- Being involved in a distressing relationship causes stress that damages cells that fight viruses.

- Emotions can be contagious. When we surround ourselves with upbeat people, we often are more so ourselves. When we surround ourselves with sad people, it can affect our emotional states in a negative way.

- Friends and business partners are crucial to our success. Spending time with those who communicate authentically with us and challenge us to stretch ourselves are the key to our growth and confidence.

Notes

"I long to accomplish some great and noble task,
but it is my chief duty to accomplish small tasks
as if they were great and noble."
—Helen Keller

Chapter Nine

LIVING YOUR PASSION

WHAT DO YOU DO for a living? Is it something that truly excites you? Something that feeds your soul? Something that allows you to use your best talents? When you get up in the morning, are you thankful for the life you have and how you get to spend your days? Can you honestly say you "love" what you do?

If your answers are yes, you are sadly atypical, and you can skip right on to the next chapter of this book. If your answers are no, you are not alone; not by a long shot.

When I worked in the marketing department of a law firm, I participated in an interview for a summer intern. My colleague and I asked the candidate why she wanted to work in a law firm, and she told us that she thought she wanted to be a lawyer. When we asked why she wanted to be a lawyer, the candidate went into a diatribe about how her parents were divorced, and her estranged father told her she would never amount to anything.

She wanted to be a lawyer, she told us, so she could say "In your face!" to her father. She wanted to show him she could be something great, and a lawyer seemed like a career that would impress him and make him feel bad about all the negative things he said to her. Not only did she not get the job, but I left the interview feeling sad for that candidate. To choose a career in order to hurt someone else is setting yourself up for misery.

Some people think what they would love to do every day is impractical. But if you love an activity, and you are good at it, you can make an occupation out of it. I once watched a television program about a person who was a professional chocolate truffle taster. She traveled the world tasting chocolate truffles, and she made them herself too. I love chocolate, so I thought I would love that job.

So I thought more about what would be involved in being a professional chocolate truffle taster. I would probably need some kind of culinary degree with a major in desserts, I guessed. As a self-described chocoholic, I would likely have to plan my eating very carefully, or I'd end up obese. If I traveled for this job, I would love the sites but would miss my family. I decided I was not passionate enough about this endeavor to do what was needed to pave the way for me to pursue it.

But how many of us could be very happy being a PR or HR person working on a cruise ship, for instance? I once met someone who wanted to travel the world, and her job was a PR director for a cruise ship. She loved it!

Sometimes we just don't think far enough out of the box, even though many of us think of ourselves as creative types. How can you marry your communication skills to something you really love—like chocolate or cruise ships or sky diving or roller coasters or your religion?

If you live and work in a way that capitalizes on your passion, then what you will communicate to others involves something you absolutely love. How you say what you say harkens back to the research I shared from Albert Mehrabian. The more conviction, or passion, the person has toward a message, which he or she will convey through body language, the more we like that person. Essentially, if we attempt to deliver a message with the sincere passion we feel for the subject, we have a greater chance of becoming more likeable. If people like you, they are more likely to listen to what you have to share.

I have heard many times, "Do what you love, and the money will follow." But many people I have coached have told me they have no idea what their passion is. I can imagine that not everyone has one defining moment in which their passion presents itself in grand form, striking like a lightning bolt so it suddenly becomes very clear what a particular person's purpose is in life. Many people live much of their lives in a job, any job, and don't especially enjoy what they do every day.

So how does one find his or her passion?

There are many great books on the subject, such as *What Color Is Your Parachute?* by Richard Nelson Bolles, *I Could Do Anything If I Only Knew What It Was: How To Discover What You Really Want and How To Get It* by Barbara Sher and *Backing U!: A Business-Oriented Guide to Backing Your Passion and Achieving Career Success* by Vaughan Evans.

The Myers-Briggs Type Indicator, which is an online questionnaire that helps measure psychological preferences and how a person makes decisions, can prove helpful as well.

To begin to discover what you love, it can be useful to think back to your childhood and re-discover who you were as a child.

When we are young, we are pure and real and courageous. We do what we do because we love it, and we don't care what anyone thinks about it (until we become teenagers of course!).

When I was in fourth grade, I remember an assignment where we were to draw pictures about what we wanted to be when we grew up, and then cut out our class pictures of our faces and glue them onto our drawings. I drew a picture of a school and drew myself as a teacher. My two younger sisters and I often played school at home, and I was always the teacher who prepared lessons, created worksheets for them to complete, and administered tests. Although I never became a full-time schoolteacher, I have spent much of my life teaching. I have taught Sunday school since I was a teenager, I have served as president of many associations throughout much of my professional life, I am a lector who shares Bible readings on Sundays in my church, and I also taught as a visiting professor at Ohio University's Scripps School of Journalism in 2006 and 2007. I currently conduct workplace training, facilitate leadership and communication workshops, and give speeches as a leadership consultant.

Because I dreamed of being a teacher back then doesn't mean that the occupation was necessarily my destiny. Rather, I think it was clear that I enjoyed teaching others, which can take many forms such as those I previously mentioned. Teaching is certainly a passion of mine, and the fact that it can be part of my career definitely helps me continue feeling passionate about what I do. I don't spend every day teaching, and I most certainly enjoy other things about what I do, but teaching is something that feeds my soul.

When we are kids, we also tend to gravitate to things at which we excel, or our natural talents. Teaching was one of mine. Many of these natural talents can develop into hobbies. That's another great place to look for your passion. Do you have any hobbies? What part of the hobby really makes you happy and why?

I remember a human resources class I took during my master's program at Ohio State where the professor drew a Venn Diagram on the white board. A Venn Diagram is a visual representation showing the similarities and differences between concepts. When you draw it, you overlap two or three circles so that any shared characteristics are represented in the overlapping portion of the circles. If memory serves, the diagram's three circles were labeled Talent, Passion, and Sales. The professor explained that if you can find what you are really good at (Talent), and what you really love to do (Passion), and what products or services you could sell to others (Sales), in the overlapping portion in the center of the diagram, that is the career that could be most satisfying and lucrative for you. He asked us if our current career fit into the center of the diagram, and many students laughed. He encouraged us to think about this Venn Diagram and to pursue a career that would fit into the center so we could live our passion.

I have always thought of my career as being framed by my Christianity. I have tried to live my life to honor God by best using the talents He gave me. Part of my challenge along the way has been discovering what talents He gave me, accepting them humbly, and using them to serve others, so that I am living in a way that I think most honors God. This is not easy, and I have had to have great courage along the way. I have done many things scared, feeling certain I was honoring God by pursuing what I felt He had in mind for me. I believe that if you consider approaching your passion in this way, it can be very fulfilling for you and valuable for those you serve.

Chapter Nine—Key Points

-   If you love an activity, and you are good at it, you can make an occupation out of it.

-   To begin to discover your passion, it can be useful to think back to our childhood and re-discover who we were as children. When we are kids, we tend to gravitate to things at which we excel, or our natural talents.

-   If you can find what you are really good at (Talent), and what you really love to do (Passion), and what products or services you could sell to others (Sales), in the overlapping portion in the center of the Venn Diagram is the career that could be most satisfying and lucrative for you.

Notes

"The leaders I met, whatever walk of life they were from, whatever institutions they were presiding over, always referred back to the same failure—something that happened to them that was personally difficult, even traumatic, something that made them feel that desperate sense of hitting bottom—as something they thought was almost a necessity. It's as if at that moment the iron entered their soul; that moment created the resilience that leaders need."
—Warren Bennis

Chapter Ten

MAKING MISTAKES

DO YOU KNOW THAT inventor Thomas Edison "failed" 10,000 times before he successfully found a proper filament to produce a working light bulb? When asked how he could find the courage to continue trying after failing so many times, Edison told a reporter, "These weren't failures. I successfully found 10,000 ways that didn't work."

Abraham Lincoln, one of our most revered Presidents, also failed many times. He failed in the grocery business and incurred a serious debt. He failed at a senatorial bid in 1856. In 1858, Lincoln was the Republican choice for the Senate seat held by Stephen Douglas. He lost that race, and Douglas kept the seat. Lincoln was not even a very experienced national politician in 1860, when he became President, but his good humor and willingness to take criticism earned him the trust and admiration of many political leaders of the time.

Lincoln personifies my concept of Quiet Leadership. In an age where politicians were prone to excessively long oratories, Lincoln spoke very simply and eloquently. He was not boisterous, as so many politicians are today, but quiet and thoughtful. He listened intently to others, and he made slow, strategic decisions. He spoke after much thought, not every chance he got. Unlike some politicians today who have big egos and pretend they know everything, Lincoln went to great lengths to surround himself with people he thought were smarter than him. He challenged himself to keep learning, and he knew he could only grow from listening to the masters of the day. His failures only motivated him to try harder and work smarter.

Orville and Wilbur Wright, credited with inventing and building the world's first successful airplane, also failed many times. They took baby steps with their invention, focusing on successfully gliding, instead of developing a powerful engine as their competitors did. Wilbur incorrectly believed a tail was not necessary for a plane early in their experimentation, and their first two gliders did not have one. Later in their trials, they endured weeks of delays caused by broken propeller shafts during engine tests. Successive flight attempts also failed, causing minor damage to their flyer, before they recorded their first flight, which lasted a whopping 12 seconds. (You have to start somewhere!)

So what can we learn from these tenacious leaders? First, we learn that if we want to achieve greatness, we must fail. Failing is an integral part of the process of doing something amazing. Second, we must look at the success hidden in each failure. Like Edison's approach, we don't have to focus on the failure, but rather what we can learn from what did not work. When you look at it as Edison did, the failure is truly a success. I think too many times we simply wallow in the failure, which of course gets us nowhere. Third, we learn that perseverance pays off. When we do something incorrectly many times, and yet we continue to learn and try new ways, we will eventually succeed. It depends, again, upon how badly we want it.

The way I approach new things, and this may work for you, is to anticipate that I will make some mistakes. If I am trying something new, I tell myself, "I will make some mistakes, and that's okay. I will learn from them and will do better the next time. The next time I will also make mistakes, but again, I will learn from them."

When you expect to make mistakes, and you accept them as necessary to achieving your ultimate goal, it relieves a lot of pressure in the situation. Yes, we all want to do our best, and we will still strive for perfection, but we will also approach situations with eyes wide open to the fact that we are only human and cannot be excellent at everything we try the first time we attempt it.

Chapter Ten — Key Points

- If we want to achieve greatness, we must fail. Failing is an integral part of the process of doing something amazing.

- We must look at the successes hidden in each failure.

- Perseverance pays off. When we do something incorrectly many times, and yet we continue to learn and try new ways, we will eventually succeed.

- When you expect to make mistakes, and you accept them as necessary to achieving your ultimate goal, it relieves a lot of pressure in the situation.

Notes

> "I do not promise you ease. I do not promise comfort. But I do promise you these: hardship, weariness, and suffering. And with them, I promise you victory."
> —Giuseppe Garibaldi

Chapter Eleven

CREATING A PLAN TO ACHIEVE GOALS

THEY SAY THE DIFFERENCE between dreams and reality is a plan. You can dream all you want about how you want your life to be, but until you make specific plans and carry them out, your vision will still be just that, a vision.

So what keeps us from taking action? Most of the time, it's fear.

I have a friend who says "Get the 'how' out of there." What he means by that is not to worry about how you will do something. Just focus on what you want to achieve, and start taking the baby steps necessary to achieve the goal. Many of us crush our dreams before they even germinate fully, don't you agree?

Let's use the goal of writing a book about leadership for communicators, for example. We may say to a friend, "I think I'll write this book." The friend is impressed, and responds, "That's great! What will it be about?" Then you say, "Maybe a book for communicators about leadership." And the conversation continues. Then, months later, you may mention to that same friend, "Yah, I've still been thinking about writing that book. I have some good ideas; I just haven't put them on paper yet." And similar scenes play out for months as the dream continues to germinate in your brain—and yet you haven't written a word, and you may never write a word of the book. Why is that?

Most of the time when procrastination is involved, the answer is fear.

Ask yourself, "What am I afraid of?" Perhaps, in this example, you fear that nobody will read the book. You may fear that when others read the book, they will not understand it or appreciate it. Maybe you think your friends will think you are pompous because you are trying to teach others something you think you know well. Maybe they will think you are an idiot because the ideas you present in the book are too simplistic. Perhaps you think you just can't do it—it's overwhelming to you to think of the time and energy involved throughout the process. Maybe you are not sure how to go about it. You know how to write, but you have no idea how to get a book published or how to sell it.

We all have fears. They are different for each of us, of course, but we all have them. Dan Millman, former world-champion athlete, university coach, martial arts instructor, and college professor, once said, "Your fears are not walls, but hurdles. Courage is not the absence of fear, but the conquering of it." We must make a choice to face our fears and, because they scare us, we have to make plans to deal with these emotions in order to achieve our goals.

So how passionate are you about a particular goal?

I wrote about passion earlier. Sometimes we are just curious about an idea and, if given time to think it through logically, we realize we aren't passionate enough to make a plan to achieve it.

Where does your passion lie? What will you allow to take up your valuable time and resources? What would you fight a pack of hungry lions to achieve?

Chapter Eleven — Key Points

–   You can dream all you want about how you want your life to be, but until you make specific plans and carry them out, your vision will still be just that, a vision.

–   Most of the time, fear keeps us from taking action to complete goals. A potential solution is to not worry about how you will do something. Just focus on what you want to achieve, and start taking the baby steps necessary to achieve the goal.

Notes

> "Whatever the mind can conceive and
> believe it can achieve."
> —Napoleon Hill

Chapter Twelve
CHALLENGE YOURSELF

ARE YOU STRETCHING YOURSELF personally and professionally? Only you can know this answer.

Sometimes we mindlessly coast, sometimes we challenge ourselves appropriately, and sometimes we overwhelm ourselves.

When you decide you want to get in shape, for instance, you can continue to sit on your couch and eat chips (coasting), you can begin walking a few miles each day (challenge), or you can run a marathon (overwhelm).

We have to be realistic about what we can achieve and be strategic about how we will keep ourselves accountable to achieve our goals.

Sitting on the couch eating chips is how many of us get through life. We find a job, we do it well, and we continue to do it well for as long as they will have us. There is fear attached to trying new things— fear of failure, fear of looking stupid, fear of being misunderstood. It is impossible to live without fear; it is part of all of us.

The key is choosing to face the fear and doing things scared. When you challenge yourself in this way, in well-measured steps that are not overwhelming, you may make mistakes initially, but once you succeed your confidence grows enormously.

Like many people, I used to be deathly afraid of public speaking. In ninth grade, my English teacher made us read one book every week, and on Fridays we would stand in front of the class, behind a lectern, and deliver our book report to our peers. Thank goodness for the lectern—my legs would shake like a pair of pantyhose hanging on a clothesline! My condition improved throughout the year. After that, I focused on my shortness of breath. According to friends, my nervousness never showed, but I certainly felt it on the inside because my heart always pounded like a jackhammer.

I remember one speech I gave in school had to be delivered on the stage of our theater. Although I remember having to do the speech, I must confess that I lost my place during the presentation, my mind went blank, and I believe I made several points multiple times before winging a wrap up statement. I don't remember seeing anyone in the audience—I was truly in a blurry fog. I don't remember anything I said after I lost my place in my notes, and I presume I had honest-to-goodness stage fright that day. I'm only grateful I didn't completely freeze and say nothing. My friends said I did well, and I did receive a good grade, but I have no idea what actually came out of my mouth.

That experience scared me so profoundly that I vowed to do everything I could to ensure I would never feel that way again. From there, I tried out for plays, signed up to be a lector at my church, taught Sunday school, and put myself in front of people as often as possible. I gave myself many chances to fail, so I could ultimately succeed.

To reduce fear we must practice those things that scare us most.

I still find it difficult to believe that I not only conduct workplace training and speak at conferences on a regular basis, but I have actually taught public speaking skills to clients. I LOVE public speaking! I'm so glad I had the opportunity to fail so many times.

So what scares you? What fear prevents you from getting what you really want? And what are you going to do about it?

Chapter Twelve — Key Points

—   When you face your fears and do things scared, taking well-measured steps that are not overwhelming, you may make mistakes initially, but once you succeed your confidence will grow enormously.

—   To reduce fear we must practice those things that scare us most.

Notes

> "If you want to (be a leader) in any kind of
> long term, committed way, you will need a vision
> that is truly your own—one that is deep and
> tenacious and that lies close to the core of who
> you believe yourself to be, what you value in
> your life, and where you see yourself going. Only
> the strength of such a dynamic vision and the
> motivation from which it springs can possibly keep
> you on this path year in and year out."
> —Jon Kabat-Zinn

Chapter Thirteen
LEADING FROM THE INSIDE OUT

SO MANY OF US try to lead from the outside in. We dress for success, we try to say all the right things, we attempt to do our work perfectly, and we read a bunch of books so we have all the answers. Then we sit back and wonder why our lives are a mess.

It's a mess because we are leading from the outside, when all of the answers to success are actually on the inside. We can do anything for a while. We can stick to a diet; we can stop being sarcastic; we can quit smoking; we can think positively. But if we don't truly own our actions and understand and accept our motivation to change, it's all a big façade.

I find that many people don't want to take responsibility for their actions. It's so much easier to point a finger at someone else. The problem is that we can't change others. We can't make someone else behave in a certain way. We can only change our own behaviors and our responses to others.

The way we change both our behaviors and our responses is to know ourselves intimately—on the inside. The more we know about ourselves, the better we understand not only when someone is pushing our buttons, but the origin of those buttons.

Why do we feel what we feel in a certain moment, when nobody else in the room is feeling that same way?

It's part of the beauty of being unique, and it's part of the challenge in communicating with others. We all have different buttons to be pushed. When we know ourselves well, and can identify our buttons and where we got them, we tend to react less and to choose our words and actions more carefully when our buttons are pushed. When people don't get what they expect to get from us, they cannot possibly give us the same response they usually give in return.

For example, let's say I usually yell at my business partner when I'm frustrated with something he's done, causing him to yell back at me. But one day I calmly explain why I'm frustrated with him instead of yelling. It's very likely he won't yell.

I wrote earlier that we can't change others. Although this is true, if we make positive changes in ourselves and then behave in more productive ways toward others, it's probable that we can influence new behaviors in others as a result.

In order to succeed long-term, we must lead from the inside out. To do this, we must know ourselves.

You learn about yourself by graciously accepting feedback from others, striving to become more emotionally aware, associating with those who challenge and support you, listening intently to others, caring for yourself, and loving who you are at this moment with all your failings. You are special and unique. There is only one you in the whole world, blessed with your distinctive talents as a communicator and leader. The more you understand and accept yourself with all your faults, the easier it is to love and accept others with all of their faults. When we listen intently and begin to understand others, and we make an effort to speak honestly and openly with others, communication suddenly becomes incredibly easier.

As you master leading from the inside out, as a Quiet Leader, you become a more powerful role model in your organization or in your business. Role models have the ability to change cultures. Remember what Gandhi said: "Be the change you wish to see in the world."

Chapter Thirteen — Key Points

–   We often lead from the outside, when all of the answers to our success are actually on the inside.

–   We can't make someone else behave in a certain way. We can only change our own behaviors and our responses to others.

–   We learn about ourselves by graciously accepting feedback from others, striving to become more emotionally aware, associating with those who challenge and support us, listening intently to others, caring for ourselves, and loving who we are at this moment with all our failings.

–   The more you understand and accept yourself with all your faults, the easier it is to love and accept others with all of their faults.

Notes

Referenced Material

1 David Rock defines "quiet leadership" as an ability to inspire high-quality thinking in your team instead of simply telling them what to do.

2 Mehrabian, A. (1971). *Silent messages*, Wadsworth, California: Belmont

3 Zamarra, J. W., Schneider, R. H., Besseghini, I., Robinson, D. K., Salerno, J. W. (1996). "Usefulness of the transcendental meditation program in the treatment of patients with coronary artery disease." *American Journal of Cardiology*, 77, 867-870.

4 Edwards, D. L. (1991). "A meta-analysis of the effects of meditation and hypnosis on measures of anxiety." *Dissertation Abstracts International*, 52 (2-B), 1039-1040; and Miller, J., Fletcher, K., & Kabat-Zinn, J. (1995). "Three-year follow-up and clinical implications of a mindfulness-based intervention in the treatment of anxiety disorders." *General Hospital Psychiatry*, 17, 192-200..

5 Kabat-Zinn, J. (1982). "An outpatient program in behavioral medicine for chronic pain patients based on the practice of mindfulness meditation: Theoretical considerations and preliminary results." *General Hospital Psychiatry*, 4, 33-47

6 Gelderloos, P., Walton, K., Orme-Johnson, D., & Alexander, C. (1991). "Effectiveness of the transcendental meditation program in preventing and treating substance misuse: A review." *International Journal of the Addictions*, 26 (3), 293-325.

7 Speca, M., Carlson, L., Goodey, E. & Angen, M. (2000). "A randomized wait-list controlled clinical trial: The effect of a mindfulness meditation-

based stress reduction program on mood and symptoms of stress in cancer outpatients." *Psychosomatic Medicine, 62,* 613-622.

8   Reibel, D.K., Greeson, J. M., Brainar, G. C., & Rosenzweig, S. (2001). "Mindfulness-based stress reduction and health-related quality of life in a heterogeneous patient population." *General Hospital Psychiatry,* 23 (4); and Williams, A., Kolar, M. M., Reger ,B. E., Pearson, J. C. (2001). "Evaluation of a wellness-based mindfulness stress reduction intervention: A controlled trial." *American Journal of Health Promotion,* 15(6), Jul-Aug 2001, 422-432; and Kabat-Zinn, J, Lipworth, L, & Burney, R. (1985). "The clinical use of mindfulness meditation for the self-regulation of chronic pain." *Journal of Behavioral Medicine,* 8, 163-190.

9   The results of this study by researchers D.S. Berry, J.W. Pennebaker, B.A. Esterling, M.H. Antoni, M.A. Fletcher, S. Margulies and N. Schneiderman are detailed in the book *Cheap Psychological Tricks: How to Get What You Want and Be Happy* by Perry W. Buffington, Ph.D.

10 Daniel Goleman describes Cacioppo's research in the book *Social Intelligence: The Revolutionary New Science of Human Relationships.*

Acknowledgments

I WANT TO THANK my amazing ILS clients, both past and present. Their desire and courage to become better people, more effective executives, and to communicate with honesty and humility inspires me every day. It is a great honor for me to be a small part of your journey.

Sincere thanks to my incredible husband, Bob, for his understanding of my independence and entrepreneurial spirit. Your support of all the new adventures I have pursued during our 20+ years of marriage and your sound advice has helped me become the person I am. I love you with all my heart, and I thank God for every day we are blessed to be together.

My wonderful sons, Carson and Connor Clark, have been instrumental in helping me identify my own opportunities for personal growth. By striving to listen to and respect them despite their youth, I feel I have learned so many valuable, life-long lessons. I love you forever, boys, and I very much appreciate the pure joy you bring to my life.

Steve Anderson suggested I write a book years ago, and I thank him for his encouragement and unwavering confidence in my abilities. Absolutely loving what you do for a living is a great blessing. Thanks, Steve, for allowing me to live my passion through ILS. I also thank my ILS colleagues, Char Anderson, Nancy Rummel, Katie Sprague, and Kim Radison, for their support. I especially thank Nancy for her early editorial help and thoughtful suggestions, and Katie for re-reading sections and offering her excellent advice.

I thank my two best friends, Pam Ray and Julie Theado. A few years back over a glass of wine, we each verbalized one main goal we hoped to achieve. Mine was to write this book. Since then, we have supported one another in pursuit of those goals. Pam and Julie have been ongoing sources of love and light in my life. I love you both very much, and I feel immensely blessed to have you both in my life.

My parents and in-laws are excellent role models in my life. Thank you Mary Condon, my Mom; Saint Joe, the name I call my Dad who passed away; and John and Janet Clark, who have all modeled honesty, hard work, courage, and perseverance. I love you all and appreciate every day I am blessed to have you in my life. I thank my siblings: Pat, Kelly, Joyce, Dee Dee, Donna, John, Leeny, Mike, Kevin, Bernie, Romie, Jo Ann (our angel), Jean, and Carol. I love you and appreciate your support, encouragement, and advice through the years.

Lastly, I thank the close friends I've made through many years of membership in the Public Relations Society of America. Being a PRSA member has greatly affected my life and my career. I thank all PRSA members past and present from whom I have received encouragement and learned many things, especially: Todd Bailey; Kathy Baird, APR; Katie Benton; Zack Bingham; Michelle Bretscher, APR; Susie Buchanan; Bruce Cadwallader; Frank Deaner, APR; Billy Fischer; Doug Frazier, APR; Kerry Francis, APR; Mary Garrick; Joe Gollehon, APR; Tammy Grimes; Jessica Hamlin; Erin Hawk, APR; Dr. Steve Iseman, APR, Fellow PRSA; Angela Krile; John Kompa, APR; Susan Mantey; Aaron Miller, Maureen Miller; Susan Merryman, APR; Vince McMorrow, APR; Dan Orzano; Amy Peach, APR; John Palmer; Jill Rako; Eileen Scahill; Denise Shively, APR; Dan Steinberg, APR; Jaron Terry, APR; Jeanne Tranter; Melissa Weber; Beth Watkins.

About the Author

M.J. CLARK RECEIVED A master's degree in organizational communication from The Ohio State University in 2006, and a bachelor's degree in journalism with a focus on public relations from the E.W. Scripps School of Journalism at Ohio University in 1995.

M.J. was a public information officer for the Ohio Department of Public Safety and then held management positions in the marketing departments at a number of Columbus, Ohio, law firms before starting her own communications consulting business in 2003. She also taught public relations classes as a visiting professor at Ohio University in 2006 and 2007. She is Accredited in Public Relations through the Public Relations Society of America.

In 2006 M.J. joined Integrated Leadership Systems (ILS), which focuses on leadership training, motivational speaking, executive coaching, and consulting. Through organizational development and one-on-one executive coaching, M.J. helps clients become better communicators in their businesses and personal lives. ILS is based in Columbus, Ohio, and serves companies all over North America.

For more information about ILS, visit www.integratedleader.com.

Notes

Notes